Bob Mc Geady has been involved in the Planning and Local Government field for over 30 years. He initially spent 17 years working for various local authorities. In that time he has dealt with a multitude of planning matters ranging from large-scale retail and housing developments to discrete one off proposals. He moved to Private Practice in 2000 and was a partner and Head of Planning and Commercial Property in Kester Cunningham John, leading a team that deals with all aspects of commercial development. He continues to act for local authorities as well as private clients and objectors, and regularly provides training sessions for officers and members of various local authorities as well as speaking at events organised by such bodies as the Local Government Group and the Royal Town Planning Institute and MBL Seminars.

Bob was an Independent Board Member of a large regional housing association and chaired a regional homelessness charity. He retains his association with Kester Cunningham John (now Ashton KCJ) as a consultant. In the Legal 500 and Chambers Directory he is rated as a leading individual for planning in East Anglia. Clients also say that he 'has a valuable insight into the attitudes and even the politics of planners'

Chambers and Partners Directory said of Meyric Lewis that "What Meyric Lewis doesn't know about planning law isn't worth knowing". He is listed as a Leader at the Bar in Chambers Directory and as a Leading Junior in the Legal 500. He specialises in all aspects of planning and compulsory purchase both at inquiries and in the courts at all appellate levels. Clients range from substantial developers to public authorities and individual developers or objectors.

Covid-19 and the Implications for Planning Law – The Essential Guide

Covid-19 and the Implications for Planning Law – The Essential Guide

Bob Mc Geady B.A. (Hons) Dip. L.G.
Solicitor (Retired)
Consultant Planning and local government related matters

Meyric Lewis BA (Hons)
Diploma in Law
Barrister

Law Brief Publishing

Published 2020 by Law Brief Publishing, an imprint of Law Brief Publishing Ltd
30 The Parks
Minehead
Somerset
TA24 8BT

www.lawbriefpublishing.com

Paperback: 978-1-913715-14-4

PREFACE

The impact of the Covid-19 virus has left us living in uncertain times. For many life has changed and will never be the same again. The question that is now uppermost is how we will react to the changes that have been forced upon us. It is not necessarily all doom and gloom as there will be opportunities as well as challenges going forward.

Planning cannot exist in isolation as all of the actions that are taken will have an impact on how we look at planning in the future. A lot of employees will be wondering why they should continue to endure the daily commute whilst a lot of employers will be looking at potential cost savings in relation to expensive bricks and mortar. Homeowners will be asking themselves whether the lack of garden or other amenities is something they are prepared to endure. All of that will impact on how we plan for the future.

This book looks forward at some of the planning issues that we will have to confront as a society. We consider the short, medium and long-term implications of the impact of virus on what planning will have to do to meet the new challenges.

The law described in this book is believed to be correct on 12 June 2020.

Stop press: The Government has announced on 22 June 2020 that (under measures yet to be published) planning permission deadlines will be extended so that "sites with consent that have an expiry date between the start of lockdown and the end of this year will now see their consent extended to 1 April 2021" see at https://www.gov.uk/government/news/new-plans-to-get-britain-building-in-coronavirus-recovery

It is also suggested that planning appeals will be sped up. So the sections below on keeping planning permission alive and planning appeals need to be read with that in mind.

Bob Mc Geady
Meyric Lewis
June 2020

CONTENTS

PART ONE

IMMEDIATE ISSUES

CHAPTER ONE
PLANNING APPLICATIONS AND PERMISSIONS

Backlog of applications and appeals

Under the new "flexibility" regulations under the Coronavirus Act 2020 allowing for remotely held Council meetings, planning decisions are still being made by local authority planning committees, see now the Local Authorities and Police and Crime Panels (Coronavirus) (Flexibility of Local Authority and Police and Crime Panel Meetings) (England and Wales) Regulations 2020. But it is to be borne in mind that only relatively few applications go to committee in any event. The question arises how overworked planning departments will be able to cope with getting existing, never mind new applications to be decided. It will be interesting to see what steps are taken over the next months and weeks to tackle the backlog. **(And see stop press in the Preface.)**

Government guidance encourages developers to agree extensions of time where necessary (without altering the time limits for determination of applications in the DMPO) but retaining the timescales means there is still the option to appeal to the Secretary of State on the grounds of non-determination, see generally at https://www.gov.uk/guidance/coronavirus-covid-19-planning-update#validation-of-applications.

This pressure will be increased by inevitable requests to vary section 106 agreements because of viability issues which we discuss below.

A lot of planning appeals have stalled or been postponed although the Inspectorate is still requiring compliance with procedural timetables. The Planning Bar is trying to keep things moving by using remote conferencing technology. But progress is not as rapid as could be wished. Unaccompanied site visits have restarted and appeals are now being determined again but not at a rate that will keep up with demand.

It will be interesting to see what steps are taken over the next months and weeks to tackle the backlog.

Keeping Planning Permission Alive

None of the Government's Covid relief measures have (at present at least) resulted in any extension to the lifetime of planning permissions for England and Wales. **Although see stop press in the Preface referring to proposed Government measures – as yet unspecified – to extend planning permission deadlines.** By contrast Scotland – which NB is outside the remit of this book – has introduced a blanket extension of 12 months for implementation of planning permissions (and for submissions for reserved matters approval) of twelve months for permissions due to expire within six months of the passing of the relevant legislation.

Equally, there have been no moves on the part of Government to reintroduce measures for the extension of the lifetime of planning permissions comparable to those in the (now superseded) Town and Country Planning (General Development Procedure) (Amendment No. 3) (England) Order 2009 which was brought in to "save" various permissions which were at risk of lapsing in the economic downturn which bit in 2008.

So the position remains for the time being that people with the benefit of planning permission still need to implement them within the specified time limit (generally three years for full planning permission and for submission of reserved matters – although NB five years for the former in Wales – and implementation of outline permissions within two years of approval of reserved matters).

So it follows that those permissions will expire if no action is taken to keep them alive. Equally, because of the effect of section 73(5) of the 1990 Act, which prevents an application to vary conditions from actually extending the lifetime of the permission, no application to extend time can be made under section 73.

Submitting reserved matters for approval may be less of an issue. But anyone in possession of a full permission or a reserved matters approval due to expire will have to take steps to implement it before the deadline.

This may well require discharge of all conditions – and fundamentally so if any of the conditions are conditions precedent in the "Whitley" form, ie the form of condition "no development shall be carried out until…" which prevents lawful implementation unless and until its requirements have been discharged, see generally *FG Whitley v. Secretary of State [1992] 3 PLR 72.* It may be possible to argue that the requirements of the condition do not go to the heart of the permission and/or it can be construed as merely requiring something to be done before development commences, see further *R (Hart Aggregates Ltd) v. Hartlepool BC [2005] JPL 1602* and subsequent cases. But that cannot by any means be taken for granted.

Close liaison will be required with officers of the local planning authority to ensure that there is a prospect of achieving discharge sufficiently swiftly to allow time for implementation before the deadline.

Assuming there are no other obstacles, the actual act of implementation may not require a great deal to constitute commencement of development so as to implement it effectively, compare the list of "material operations" for the commencement of development in section 56 of the 1990 Act, namely,

> "(a) any work of construction in the course of the erection of a building;
>
> (aa) any work of demolition of a building;
> (b) the digging of a trench which is to contain the foundations, or part of the foundations, of a building;
>
> (c) the laying of any underground main or pipe to the foundations, or part of the foundations, of a building or to any such trench as is mentioned in paragraph (b);
>
> (d) any operation in the course of laying out or constructing a road or part of a road;
>
> (e) any change in the use of any land which constitutes material development".

In *Malvern Hills DC v. Secretary of State [1982] JPL 439*, the predecessor of section 56 was stated to be "a benevolent section which is aimed at avoiding hardship to a developer who is genuinely undertaking the development" and that "very little need be done to satisfy the section". Also, the list of material operations given above has been said not to be exhaustive, see *Field v. First Secretary of State [2004] EWHC 147 (Admin).*

Therefore, so long as a workforce can be mustered in sufficient time to carry out the necessary task of implementation, then a permission could be saved. It is nevertheless advisable to document and evidence any works of commencement to protect the position for the future. Also, and for the avoidance of doubt, it is important to implement the permission substantially in accordance with its actual terms, see eg *Commercial Land Ltd v. Secretary of State [2003] JPL 358.*

However, regrettably, if lawful implementation cannot be achieved before the deadline, the holder of the permission will have to re-apply for it. This may raise issues of changes in policy in the interval since the original permission was granted and may also have implications for the viability of any scheme.

It is therefore earnestly to be hoped that urgent steps will be taken by the Government to pass legislation extending the lifetime of permissions.

CHAPTER TWO
ENFORCEMENT ISSUES

The same as for deadlines for implementation of planning permissions, time does not cease to run for taking enforcement action. The same applies to deadlines for appealing against enforcement notices.

There may however be some potential for flexibility from the point of view of those who are required to comply with the requirements of an enforcement notice which has taken effect but where lockdown has resulted in difficulties with complying within the specified time period.

Time limits for taking enforcement action

The three main time limits for taking enforcement action are set out in section 171B of the 1990 Act. For operational development (i.e. building and other operations), the time limit is four years from substantial completion. Similarly, where there has been a breach of planning control consisting in the change of use of any building to use as a single dwellinghouse, no enforcement action may be taken after the end of the period of four years beginning with the date of the breach. In the case of "any other breach of planning control" (ie material changes of use and breaches of planning conditions), no enforcement action may be taken after the end of the period of ten years beginning with the date of the breach.

For completeness we would note that the time limit is also four years where the breach of planning control involved is change of use to a single dwelling house contrary to a condition prohibiting such a change, see *Arun District Council v Secretary of State* [2006] EWCA

Civ 1172. (We discuss such matters further in our other work Certificates of Lawful Use and Development: A Guide to Making and Determining Applications).

In a case where the four year time limit applies for operational development which was substantially completed a bit under four years ago, time will continue to tick away so that immunity from enforcement action, at least where the operational development in the form of, say, a built structure is concerned, will accrue. (It is to be noted however that the potential still exists for enforcement action to be taken to require cessation of use where ten years' immunity has not been secured, even though the structure would be allowed to remain, see *Sumner v Secretary of State* [2010] EWHC 372 (Admin) – although note reference in the *Welwyn Hatfield* case referred to below to "principles of fairness and good governance [potentially precluding enforcement action] to render the building useless", see per Lord Mance at para. 17).

But while time will continue to run so that local planning authorities may not have been able to take enforcement action before immunity from enforcement action is acquired in the case of material changes of use or use in breach of condition, it may well be various businesses carried on at premises which were forced to shut down because of the national lockdown will not be able to prove the requisite continuity of use of the relevant period.

This because there is no such thing as a presumption of continuance in planning i.e. where a use is presumed to continue even though it is not actually occurring see eg *Secretary of State v Thurrock BC* [2002] 2 PLR 43 and *Swale BC v Secretary of State* [2006] JPL 886. Therefore, some businesses that have been operating without permission are in danger of being unable to acquire lawful status if they stop even temporarily.

NB though that there should not be the same problem for those taking advantage of the single dwellinghouse provision, assuming they were in residence continuously during lockdown, because their continuity of use in breach of planning control would not be interrupted. (Although the position would very likely be otherwise if they lived elsewhere during the lockdown period, and compare the position of people in breach of occupancy restrictions, see *Nicholson v Secretary of State* [1998] 2 PLR 6).

It might be argued that a business is continuing as owners/employees are working from home although they are not working from the relevant building/land. But it seems unlikely that such an argument could succeed given that planning is concerned with the actual use of specific premises or land – and so if the business was carried on remotely, that would not count towards achieving immunity where the relevant premises/land were concerned.

Compare *Miles v National Assembly of Wales* [2007] EWHC 10 (Admin) which was concerned with cessation of motorbiking activities on land during the foot and mouth epidemic it was argued that the reason for the cessation of use was the statutory provisions prohibiting access to land. The landowner said that the use would have continued but for those restrictions but that did not find favour with the court.

It is an interesting question whether someone who had been carrying on a business despite the prohibitions in place under lockdown might seek to argue that they had succeeded in acquiring immunity by carrying on continuously in breach regardless. But it also seems likely that they would be caught by the principle in *Welwyn Hatfield Borough Council v Secretary of State* [2011] UKSC 15 that no one should profit from deliberate concealment of an unauthorised use.

It may also be that a local planning authority faced with such a situation could invoke the planning enforcement order provisions in section 171BA and following of the 1990 Act if the court can be satisfied that the apparent breach concerned "has (to any extent) been deliberately concealed" so that they would have extra time to take the necessary action.

It is a moot point whether someone who proclaimed brazenly that they had continued to carry on their unauthorised activities openly in defiance of lockdown could not be accused of any concealment. The question would then arise of whether the principle in *Welwyn Hatfield* of not sanctioning wrongdoing would extend to include a wilful breach of the Covid regulations imposing the lockdown.

There is a related point here that authorities will not have been in a position to keep up with general enforcement monitoring including site inspections and investigations. Time will, therefore, continue to tick away against them. But, again, the ticking of time will by and large only avail people who have substantially completed an operational development a bit under four years ago or who were continuously in occupation of an unauthorised "single dwellinghouse".

But in any event, authorities should be actively considering which enforcement cases on their files might require service of an enforcement notice to ensure that the ticking of the potential immunity clock is stopped.

Enforcement appeal deadlines

The time for appealing against an enforcement notice is "before the date specified in the enforcement notice as the date on which it is to take effect", section 174(3) of the 1990 Act.

NB that there is no provision allowing for an extension of time and so anyone who receives an enforcement notice within lockdown should not assume that they will be granted any grace or flexibility. If they wish to appeal against the notice they will have to get on with it. If they fail to do so, the notice will take effect and will have to be complied with (with the potential for criminal penalties for non-compliance).

The only conceivable alternative to this might be to make a regulatory planning application after the event (although that is unlikely to be approved) or to seek to persuade the local planning authority that the enforcement notice should be withdrawn in exercise of the power under section 173A and re-served so that the right of appeal would revive (but that is even more unlikely – unless, say, the notice could be shown to be invalid in some respect).

Where a High Court appeal under section 289 against a decision on a section 174 appeal upholding an enforcement notice is concerned, the deadline is four weeks, see CPR PD52D para. 26.1(1). Since this deadline is contained in the CPR there might be grounds for seeking an extension of time – but only if good reason could be made out for missing the deadline. Success in such an application can by no means be guaranteed.

NB on the other hand that if someone (such as the LPA or a third party objector to the appeal) wishes to "appeal against" or challenge a grant of planning permission on the section 174 appeal, then they have to challenge that "action" within six weeks of the decision, see sections 284(3)(e) and 288(4B) of the 1990 Act – and that six week time limit in non-extendable.

Time for compliance with enforcement notices

Every enforcement notice must specify time periods within which steps required for compliance with the notice must be carried out, see section 173(9) of the 1990 Act. Time limits can be successive, e.g. requiring demolition of a building within one month; then site clearance within one month after that and finally site restoration another month after that.

Obviously, lockdown could affect someone's ability to organise the labour necessary to achieve compliance in such a situation.

There is a defence in section 179(3) to a prosecution under section 179(1) for failure to comply with an enforcement notice that the person being prosecuted "did everything [they] could be expected to do to secure compliance with the notice" – and that might include having arranged to carry out the necessary steps but being frustrated by lockdown.

Similarly, if the circumstances of the case were that the local planning authority were minded to seek an injunction under section 187B of the Act, coercively to restrain the breach of planning control, then of course it would be grounds for resisting an injunction application that it was not physically possible to comply at present.

But clearly it would be preferable to avoid such a situation by requesting the local planning authority to invoke their parallel power in section 173A to "waive or relax any requirement of [an enforcement] notice and, in particular... extend [the] period specified in accordance with section 173(9)".

Indeed, we would suggest that an authority should be pro-active and sympathetic in volunteering a period of grace to those whose plans for compliance with a notice have genuinely been hampered by the lockdown unless, say there were severe ongoing impacts on amenity or the environment which warranted immediate action.

CHAPTER THREE
CIL PAYMENTS/DEMANDS

In the same way as it is desirable for there to be specific legislation to extend the life of planning permissions, there are current issues arising with CIL which are likely to present problems for developers. In fact, as of 13 May 2020, the Government has stated its intention to put in place certain (temporary) measures by way of amendment to the CIL Regulations 2010 "to give authorities more discretion to defer payment for small and medium sized developers without having to impose additional costs on them".

Prior to lockdown a number of planning permissions will have been commenced which will have given rise to a current liability to CIL under the Regulations as they stand. But in current conditions, businesses and homeowners may not have the cash to pay or may wish to retain the cash for what they would regard as more important purposes.

Enforcement of payment may be the final straw for some businesses. Homeowners may not have the ability to actually pay. Adding punitive surcharges and late payment interest under regs. 85 and 87 is not really going to help – and NB that liability for interest is automatic.

Local authorities have no ability to agree deferral of payment. Potentially, they could simply decide not enforce payments for now, although query whether the extent of any discretion they may really have in this regard, see reg. 69(1): "The collecting authority must serve a demand notice on each person liable to pay an amount of CIL in respect of a chargeable development".

Permissions will continue to be issued which will give rise to liability but only when commenced. So liability can be avoided in those limited circumstances.

We have already looked at the possibility of having to commence development in order to retain the benefit of an implemented permission. But that may not be a practical option for developers if they do not have the cash to pay the CIL liability – so they will find themselves in a Catch 22.

On 13 May 2020, the Government published guidance for local authorities on how they might reduce the burden of CIL on developers and, in particular, smaller developers who it is recognised "may need more help".

The Guidance is to be found at https://www.gov.uk/guidance/coronavirus-covid-19-community-infrastructure-levy-guidance but is largely summarised below.

The Government therefore proposes to amend the CIL regulations "in due course" to give authorities more discretion to defer payment for small and medium sized developers without having to impose additional costs on them.

The guidance refers to local authority instalment policies and refers to the fact that CIL charging authorities have the power under regulation 69B of the CIL Regs to allow those liable to CIL to pay the charge in one or more instalments and can set the date(s) on which payment is due, through publication of an "instalment policy" under reg. 69B(1).

However, where the charging authority concerned does not have an instalment policy, then the default position is that the CIL liability is payable in full at the end of the period of 60 days beginning with the intended commencement date under regulation 70(7).

It is pointed out that CIL charging authorities can bring into effect a new instalment policy at any time. However, any new instalment policy will only apply to chargeable developments commencing after the new instalment policy comes into effect. So CIL will still be payable either in accordance with any instalment policy that was already in place at the time of commencement of the chargeable development (or will be payable in full if there is/was no instalment policy).

For phased development the issue may not be so acute, since each phase will be a separate chargeable development, and so later phases that have not yet commenced could be subject to a new instalment policy. It is therefore suggested that charging authorities could take advantage of this provision to introduce new instalment policies for as-yet uncommenced chargeable phases.

The new instalment policy can come into effect on the day after it has been published on the authority's website, see reg. 69B(2)(a), and must make a copy of it available for inspection, see reg. 69B(3), which may present certain practical difficulties, unless publication on the website is taken to suffice.

Where enforcement is concerned, which we touched on above, the Guidance suggests that CIL collecting authorities have "more discretion" about how they deal with the late payment of CIL and that this could provide some scope to ease financial pressures on developers.

The guidance states that, in normal circumstances, a CIL collecting authority might consider it expedient to stop development until the outstanding amount has been paid. Under the regulations an authority can issue a CIL stop notice under reg. 90 requiring development to cease until the liability has been discharged, with potential penalties in the form of prosecution or an injunction under regs. 93 and 94. Clearly, however, decisions as to whether and when to take such enforcement actions are at the discretion of the collecting authority and they will need to consider carefully whether any such action is necessary or proportionate in the circumstances.

The guidance also refers to authorities' power to impose surcharges under reg. 85 on a person that has not paid their CIL. However, again, authorities are reminded that the imposition of surcharges is a matter within their discretion of the authority. The guidance states that authorities can therefore choose not to impose the surcharge for late payment and "are encouraged to consider using this discretion where appropriate".

As noted above, the guidance goes on to state that that late payment interest accrues automatically, starting from the day after the day payment was due, see again reg. 87. The payment is calculated at an annual rate of 2.5% above the Bank of England base rate. The guidance repeats that authorities have no discretion to "disapply" the accrual of interest and so, the Government says, in addition to the measures introduced to help businesses as a whole, they propose to help small and medium sized developers further.

They propose to do this by introducing amendments to the 2010 Regulations to enable charging authorities (1) to defer payments, (2) to temporarily disapply late payment interest and (3) to provide a discretion to return interest already charged where they consider it appropriate to do so for developers that have an annual turnover of less than £45 million. It is stated that this may include interest that has accrued in the period between the introduction of the lockdown and the regulatory changes coming into effect. It is further stated that it is not intended that these easements will be open-ended and that they will be removed when the economic situation has recovered.

The Guidance reminds us that "CIL regulations are subject to an affirmative resolution procedure, which requires debate in Parliament. However, existing flexibilities and the government's clear intention to legislate should give authorities confidence to use their enforcement powers with discretion and provide some comfort to developers that, where appropriate, they will not be charged extra for matters that were outside of their control".

Therefore, until such amendment regulations are able to take effect:

"CIL charging authorities are encouraged to consider making use of the ability to introduce an instalment policy (or amend an existing instalment policy); and

noting the government's clear intention to introduce legislation to permit deferral of CIL payments and disapply late payment interest for SMEs, CIL collecting authorities are encouraged to use their discretion in considering what, if any, enforcement action is appropriate in respect of unpaid CIL liabilities; and

CIL authorities should take a positive approach to their engagement with SME developers, to ensure CIL liabilities do not cause undue burdens over the period of disruption caused by the coronavirus".

However, the above is addressed at smaller developers and so the Guidance merely advises authorities to "note" the existing flexibilities they have around enforcing CIL for larger developers, including flexibilities over the imposition of surcharges. However, the Guidance again reminds us, "late payment interest will remain mandatory where such flexibilities are used".

The Guidance concludes by acknowledging that there is a greater margin of discretion for behaving flexibly in the context of an applicable section 106 obligation than there is under the CIL Regulations. So the Guidance encourages local authorities to consider whether it would be appropriate to allow developers to defer delivery of payments or obligations.

It is suggested that deferral periods could be time-limited, or linked to the Government's wider legislative approach and the lifting of CIL easements (although in this case we would encourage the use of a back-stop date). Deeds of variation can be used to agree any changes. It is stated that authorities should take a pragmatic and proportionate approach to the enforcement of section 106 planning obligations during this period and that this should help remove barriers for developers and minimise the stalling of sites.

So there is some reform in prospect, which is somewhat limited in scope, and is addressed directly at smaller developers. The detail of course remains to be seen.

CHAPTER FOUR
VIABILITY AND SECTION 106 AGREEMENTS

The issue of viability is both a short and medium term one to be addressed. Recent section 106 agreements which have permissions that are alive will have been negotiated on the basis of valuation assumptions that are most likely now wide of the mark. In some cases developers have walked away from sites as the landowner was not prepared to look at the option arrangements. The developers were unable to arrive at a GDV that would give them confidence to take the risk of pursing the option and developing the site. A lot of landowners are in the fortunate position that they can afford to wait and see what happens. However, that will have impacts on the deliverability of housing in line with the Government's stated desire to deliver 300,000 homes per year. Undoubtedly the need for that level of development will not have receded during the lockdown and will likely have increased with the forecast spike in Covid divorces and separations.

In other cases sites have commenced but developers have no idea at present how they will pan out. It should not necessarily be assumed that sites will automatically start up again. Even if they do there will not be the same level of intensity of development. This is due to a number of factors. At the present time housebuilders face a number of practical challenges. Following lockdown the manufacture or various raw materials such as plasterboard, timber etc closed down or reduced as well. It is not a simple exercise to turn on a tap and have these materials flow again. There is a time lag which will affect delivery. Housebuilders do not operate in a vacuum and some developers are struggling with obtaining such mundane items as carpets to complete houses. This is because carpet factories are still in lockdown as the shops that sell the bulk of their wares are still closed. When carpet shops re-open there will still be the inevitable time lag before full production is reached. That will no doubt be affected by the appetite of consumers to spend money they either do not have or that they are putting away for a rainy day.

There have already been cost increases in the construction industry. This will affect the ability of developers to deliver if asking prices cannot be sustained. In many cases viability will have to be revisited.

Of greater concern in terms of delivery and viability will be a lack of liquidity in the market. Whilst interest rates are at an historic low there is still a reluctance on the part of banks and other lenders to lend. This could result in an increase in the available interest rate that developers will have to pay to bring sites forward. That in turn will affect viability.

Viability doesn't just apply to residential development although that is usually the most affected area. It will be interesting to see the impact on the retail industry as it just be doubtful that the planning system's penchant for "enabling" retail development will be able to be so easily indulged going forward.

During the credit crunch of 2008 the vast majority of local authorities were happy to look at viability on a voluntary basis and to renegotiate agreements. These often included some form of re-evaluation of viability in the future. This is now written into the NPPF and NPPG. These clauses should now be standard in Deeds of Variation. Typically, they require a further viability assessment to be undertaken at an agreed point in the development. This needs to be at a sufficiently advanced point but also at one where there is still the ability to enforce the provisions. The provisions then go on to specify that if the profit level that has been agreed as appropriate has been exceeded then there is some form of payment to the local authority.

In setting the payment mechanism it is important to balance risk and reward so that in many cases there is a 50/50 split of the excess profit. In addition, and in order to ensure that the obligations remain as proper planning obligations the local authority should be capped at the level which equates to the amount of infrastructure/affordable housing that has been deferred. In certain instances the agreement can provide for payment of any excess profit up to the agreed level in the first instance. Either approach is acceptable and will depend upon what can be agreed in the circumstances in which the amendment is being negotiated.

As with everything in life there are always exceptions. During the last recession in order to assist developers and to force those local authorities who were refusing to act reasonably to take the issue of viability seriously the government of the day introduced section 106BA. At present we have the Guidance issued by MHCLG on 13th May 2020. This Guidance makes it clear that local authorities must act reasonably to help developers with cash flow and to defer obligations where this is possible. This is only exhortation at present and it remains to be seen whether it will be necessary to re-introduce section 106BA or something similar. Section 106BA was restricted to affordable housing. In the present circumstances it may be that a wider assessment may be required as whilst it is recognised that the provision of affordable housing has most impact on viability that may not be sufficient if we are faced with the recession being predicted at the highest levels of government.

CHAPTER FIVE
LOCAL PLANS AND DELIVERY OF DEVELOPMENT

At the time of writing sites for residential development are beginning to open again. Developers are being very cautious and whilst they would like to get back to full production there are a number of competing challenges that will impact their ability to continue to deliver homes.

As previously stated it is not simply a case of turning on the development tap as there will be lead times for raw materials and the impact of social distancing will lead to longer construction times.

In relation to local plans there are a number of questions that will become apparent as we embrace the new normal. For example,

What will be the actual demand for houses going forward? Demand will not necessarily have decreased during the Covid crisis and it may even have increased as a result of a number of different factors.

However, will existing householders feel confident about moving? Some households may have no choice but to seek to move but that doesn't necessarily mean that they will be able to. It is likely that mortgage finance will become more difficult to come by and this will have the effect of reducing demand as although households will want to move they may not qualify for mortgage finance or they may not feel comfortable taking on new debt due to the uncertain economic outlook.

As already indicated developers will not be immune to the issue of financing which will result in a delicate balance between building what can be financed and then sold.

The implications for local plans of this uncertainty could be very profound indeed. Plans are predicated and tested on the assumption of historic information as to delivery. In certain cases an element of crystal ball gazing is used where delivery rates can be assumed to differ from the historical evidence. The Housing Delivery Test has been introduced to concentrate minds on "actual" as opposed to "theoretical" delivery. Questions are being asked as to the appropriateness of this test at present given that, unlike the production of a local plan which is something over which local authorities have considerable ability to affect, local authorities could end up being in effect "punished" for a failure to deliver in circumstances where their ability to perform is constrained by external forces not of their making. It has been suggested that the test should be deferred for this year and maybe refined for subsequent years. That is fine up to a point but there are a whole host of other issues that whose impact has yet to be felt.

Some questions that occur are;

- Will there be more second-hand accommodation available as a result of the death rate caused by Covid?
- On the opposite tack will there be increased demand for accommodation as the elderly seek to remove themselves from nursing homes?
- Will there be a spike in the divorce rate leading to demand for more housing? Apparently enquiries to divorce lawyers are already increasing beyond normal expected levels.

- Will there be a baby boom resulting in a need to move to a bigger house? The opposite of the divorce issue!

- Will houses need to be bigger to accommodate the home office? There is increasing evidence that home working is becoming a much more attractive proposition for both workers and employers alike. This will comprise a combination of full time working from home and staggered attendance at the office. Some employers are looking at the cost savings that can accrue by downsizing office space. This will undoubtedly have an impact on the land allocated for employment purposes going forward.

- What about gardens and the size of houses generally? Whilst house prices are showing signs of falling there is also evidence that those with a good-sized garden are actually holding up in terms of prices. The design of housing going forward will be driven by what the market requires. Thus, if home working is to become more prevalent will that drive demand for larger houses that contain space for a home office.

Equally, it has become apparent that those who have been confined to small outdoor spaces will perhaps be demanding larger gardens.

If those two issues become the new normal then the question has to be asked as to what effect that will have on the amount of land that needs to be allocated? Further, allocating more land to take account of larger houses and gardens may not result in higher prices paid to landowners as whilst consumers may want these amenities they may not necessarily be prepared to pay a premium for them. Interesting times lie ahead.

As can be seen a lot of assumptions made when current local plans, either adopted or in course of preparation, were formulated will need to be revisited. The Government's "planning update" of 13th May for planning under Covid is that they "continue to want to see Local Plans progressing through the system". But what will the implications be for Plans already under consideration when many would say that the assumptions on which they were predicated have fundamentally changed? This will apply across the whole of the planning spectrum as will be seen when we tackle such other issues as town centres and provision of telecommunications for example.

PART TWO

MEDIUM-TERM ISSUES

CHAPTER SIX
SECTION 106 AND VIABILITY

In a laudable attempt to speed up the planning process Government to great fanfare published relevant Guidance in 2019 together with the methodology for calculating viability. Arising from this is a presumption that where there is an up to date local plan there will eb an assumption that development is viable and it will be up to individual applicants to convince local authorities that viability was an issue that needed to be dealt with at the application stage. Despite Government's rose-tinted approach to viability it was still an issue in a large number of applications. In most cases as local plans adopted prior to issue of the Guidance could not be regarded as up to date there was always going to be a time lag until plans caught up. Covid has thrown a further spanner into the works such that Government should be considering revising the Guidance to take account of the changing circumstances. RICS has undertaken some very good work in this regard and has produced mandatory guidance for RICS members to adopt when dealing with viability. However, that guidance only deals with site specific matters. That means that the guidance in relation to the approach to viability in the local plan process could do with some clarity.

When it comes to section 106 agreements and how viability is dealt with there are a number of different approaches as has already been alluded to. The authors wonder whether a standard approach to this issue for section 106 should be adopted with standard wording agreed between local authority and developer representatives. Such a clause could then become a boiler plate clause in section 106 agreements.

Viability is not the only issue for section 106 agreements. As has been seen with the CIL debacle where legislation to amend has been found to take longer than might have been considered ideal there are various delays that affect the completion of section 106 agreements. Section 106 (1) (a) proceeds on the basis that "any person interested in land…." can enter into the section 106 agreement. Local authorities rightly seek to bind various interests in the land and there is often a discussion as to whether or not a party has a sufficient interest in the land so as to require them to be a party. It could make it clear which interests qualify and which do not.

As part of any review of the CIL Regulations government should consider clarifying that only those with a defined "legal" interest in the land have to be a party. It could go further and make provision that certain classes of interest could be bound as per a statutory regime. For example, mortgagees are routinely included in section 106 agreements but their liability is then constrained so that in effect they will rarely, if ever, become subject to the terms of the section 106 agreement. Could there not be a statutory provision that sets out the liability of persons such as mortgagees which would be incorporated by operation of the statutory provisions thus time and expense in completing the section 106 agreement.

If the government were to look at amendments to section 106 it might also take the opportunity to outlaw the inclusion of "social" as opposed to "planning" or "development" matters in section 106 agreements.

A further area that is long due for consideration is the time period in which an application to amend a section 106 agreement can eb made under section 106A. The current 5-year period is not appropriate any longer especially in light of the cat that permissions have shorter lifespans than they did when the provisions were first introduced. In the present climate a period of 12 months would be more appropriate or perhaps an "at any time following completion" approach so that permissions could be issued and implemented whilst unreasonable provisions which could be agreed to get the permission issued could then be addressed by means of an appeal if necessary.

The test for deciding whether or not the obligation should also be updated so that there must be some form of useful "planning' purpose contrary to the findings in the recent case of *R (on the application of Mansfield District Council) v Secretary of State for Housing Communities & Local Government & JA Clark [2018] EWHC 1794 Admin.*

CHAPTER SEVEN REVIEW OF LOCAL PLANS

As discussed in the short-term issues section local plans and the assumptions that underpin them will need to be looked at. At present there is a backlog of plans in the course of either preparation or consideration by Inspectors. There must be a serious question mark hanging over the ability of Inspectors to make a finding that a plan is sound when we are only beginning to understand some of the implications of Covid. Certain local authorities may see this as a godsend to enable them to delay yet further the production of a plan. Others will be very keen to get a plan in place albeit that it will have to be recognised to be imperfect. Inspectors could find a plan sound but require that an early review within say, three, as opposed to 5 years, should be undertaken when the impacts of Covid become more manifest.

Whichever outcome prevails we are going to be left with an unsatisfactory situation and no doubt there will be applicants who will seek to take advantage of the situation by seeking to produce evidence that shows that the local plan, whilst adopted, does not reflect what is actually happening in the local economy. No doubt objectors will also seek to use the current hiatus as a way of seeking to frustrate development on the basis of a lower growth and delivery trajectory than had been assumed.

As with the extension of planning permissions it could be said that Government needs to come up with a short-term solution which deals with how local plans should be regarded where they are in force and what allowances, if any, Inspectors examining current plans should make for Covid.

CHAPTER EIGHT
CIL AND CHARGING SCHEDULES

Regulation 14 (1) of the Community Infrastructure Levy Regulations 2010 provides as follows;

> *"in setting rates including differential rates) in a charging schedule, a charging authority must strike an appropriate balance between-*
>
> *(a) the desirability of funding from CIL (in whole or in part) the actual and expected estimated total cost of infrastructure required ti support development of its area, taking into account other actual and expected sources of funding; and*
>
> *(b) the potential effects (taken as a whole) of the imposition of CIL on the economic viability of development across its area"*

Thus, a charging authority is unable to set a rate that renders development unviable in its area. Whilst Regulation 28 (3) (b) provides that an adopted charging Schedule remains in force until *"the end of the day before the day a revised charging schedule issued by that charging authority takes effect"* the Regulations are silent on the need for review and reassessment. Even the Planning Practice guidance is silent on this as well. As we discuss elsewhere is relation to CIL the Government needs to take account of the fact that whilst there may be a proposal to amend the Regulations to enable deferment of payments it also need to look at further amendments to require regular reviews of the levy to ensure that it is up to date and takes account of prevailing economic conditions. It is all well and good offering deferment but if a development has become unviable a deferment will not assist with bringing that development forward if ultimately the developer will be unable to afford to pay due to viability issues.

At present it would appear that many charging schedules will fail to meet the basic test set out in Regulation 14 if there were to be examined today. Going forward the situation is only likely to deteriorate further because of potential viability issues. The Regulations do provide for some possibility for relief in exceptional circumstances, see further above. However, this will require a very resource intensive exercise and the charging authority being convinced that the relief would have an unacceptable effect on development. There are potential issues with state aid to eb dealt with. In the current climate the impact of Covid has yet to fully filter through. In the medium-term Government could simply designate that Covid is an "exceptional circumstance" and provide authorities with the ability to revisit the amounts payable based on individual viability. A bit like an expanded section 106 BA as previously mentioned.

Government has been slow to bring forward amendments to the Regulations. In accordance with the communication strategy of burying certain decisions on bad news days Government might even take the opportunity to quietly drop CIL altogether given its overall lack of popularity.

PART THREE

LONGER-TERM ISSUES

CHAPTER NINE
DISCUSSION OF LONGER-TERM ISSUES

Experience tells us that once the cork has been removed from the bottle and the genie is allowed to roam freely that it is very difficult, if not impossible, for the genie to be brought back under control and the status quo restored. Thus, we have progressed very swiftly on a number of fronts that were probably inevitable at some stage but have been brought forward by Covid. Now that we have gotten used to virtual planning committees and court hearings as the current default position it will be interesting to see how much of that remains in the future. If digital communication is to become more of a norm then there will be certain parts of planning practice that will have to be rethought and we now turn to address these.

Publicity and consultation

The technology is already in use whereby applications and appeals can be submitted electronically. It is also possible to make representations electronically. The system works.

However, the system is also backed up by good old-fashioned paper consultation methods. This ensures that those who may have an interest in proposed development become aware of the proposals and are thus given an opportunity to participate if they chose to do so.

Posting of site notices are a requirement for planning applications and appeals and environmental statements and draft Local Plans have to be placed on deposit for physical inspection.

Whereas the latter might have been achievable even under lockdown, the latter could have presented a real (unless web publication alone were permissible but that is not what the relevant regulations require and depends on people having access to a computer).

But see now the exceptional temporary measures introduced in England, as from 14 May 2020, in the Town and Country Planning (Development Management Procedure, Listed Buildings and Environmental Impact Assessment) (England) (Coronavirus) (Amendment) Regulations 2020, S.I. 2020/505. The amendments made by the regulations are time limited to expire on 31 December 2020. The recently NPPG explains that these temporary measures are intended to provide flexibility under the existing system and to prevent delays, see Reference ID: 15-035-20200513. For Wales, compare Planning Applications (Temporary Modifications and Disapplication) (Wales) (Coronavirus) Order 2020 which came into force on 19 May 2020.

The challenge going forward is to find a way of ensuring that those who should know about proposed development are alerted. This will be not be easy.

A similar issue arises around digital poverty. We cannot just assume that everyone has access to the internet. True, nowadays most people do but not everyone does either through choice or circumstances. How do we enable these individuals to take part? We are all aware of the silver surfers but there are also a lot of grey landlubbers who simply cannot get to grips with the technology. As this is a generational issue it will no doubt pass but when?

The issue is not just confined to the general public. One of the things that has become apparent is that the technology available to local authorities has been found to be lacking. Indeed this has been cited as one of the reasons for the slow approach of the Planning Inspectorate to moving forward with digital hearings. This may be due to a lack of investment or simply local authorities remaining "behind the curve" in terms of technology. There have also been reports of people "trolling" or disrupting online meetings depending on the choice of software by the hosts.

As regards planning committee meetings local authorities are starting to dip their toes in the water and are using the new powers given to them under the Local Authorities and Police and Crime Panels (Coronavirus) (Flexibility of Local Authority and Police and Crime Panel Meetings) (England and Wales) Regulations 2020, S.I. 2020/392. Some have embraced the technology more than others and will make a success of it. Others will struggle as they will not be sufficiently committed. No doubt at some point there will be some form of evaluation as to what works and what doesn't so that the experience going forward can be one that is meaningful.

There are obvious issues around participation and public speaking but ways and means of dealing with this are being found on a daily basis. One of the potential advantages might be a situation where members do not feel intimidated when the hordes throng to the actual meeting. This may have knock on effects in terms of decision making. However, it might be that some will miss the obvious tension and grand theatre associated with a controversial application being dealt with live with the roar of the crowd and the smell of the greasepaint!

Reviewing of Infrastructure Projects

Much has been made by the Government in recent years about the critical importance of major infrastructure projects to the national economy. But issues such as the review of the desirability of HS2 and the legal challenge to the expansion of Heathrow Airport calls into question the assumed need for or presumed benefits inherent in these massive (and massively expensive) schemes.

We all experience the increasing tension between the sense of wishing to reduce one's carbon footprint in the face of extremes of climate conditions and, as we seem destined to slip back into recession, the expense involved in embarking on exotic holidays abroad.

Sir John Armitt, Chair of the National Infrastructure Commission, has written to the Lord Chancellor to reiterate the Commission's ongoing support through providing independent advice on all sectors of economic infrastructure (ie energy, transport, water and wastewater, waste, flood risk management and digital communications) citing three key priorities of (i) long-term productivity and competitiveness; (ii) levelling up regional inequalities and (iii) achieving net zero by 2050 or before – which will inevitably throw up competing demands and challenges, despite Sir John's view that these factors are "mutually reinforcing rather than in conflict".

The letter also encourages the Government to continue with their stated agenda of giving larger cities the funding and freedom they need to start work on local infrastructure priorities to provide regional stimulus and help meet the needs of "growing populations".

But we pose the question below what the future will be for inner cities. We also note that a number of high-profile projects which are already behind target and over budget may well not be taken forward for a long time if at all in these uncertain economic conditions.

With rail companies, airlines and other transport providers taking a hit because of massively reduced passenger numbers, how is that going to affect their budgets for future development?

If commuting is to become a thing of the past then the justification for the local and regional road improvements recently announced will become questionable.

It seems likely that there will be more objections to schemes when they are the subject of planning applications, compulsory purchase or development consent orders on the basis that they are now premature or that the underlying assumptions and justifications for them are wrong.

It is not to be doubted that the rail network is in need of improvements. However, if post-Covid there are lower levels of potential customer demand, then that will affect the cost-benefit ratios to be demonstrated to secure funding for network upgrades and development.

We are already behind in replacing existing energy generating capacity. What effect will changes such as more people working from home have? Will there be a resurgence of support for nuclear power? But if so, how (and where) might that be achieved? It may well be that Government will have to revisit the suite of existing National Policy Statements.

The current Government guidance on NSIPs states that "examinations are continuing via written/email submissions and the publication of documents online", see generally at:

https://assets.publishing.service.gov.uk/government/uploads/system/uploads/attachment_data/file/888114/COVID-19_Guidance_for_NSIP_External_Events_Advice__28_May_2020.pdf

But we note that progress in present conditions will inevitably be slow and, given the ever-worsening state of the economy, uncertain.

The future of town centres?

Town centres have changed successively over past years with continuing closures resulting in many of them being not much more than a collection of coffee outlets, mobile phone and charity shops. It is likely that, in parallel with the downsizing or outright failure of various retail chains, a lot of the businesses currently represented in town centres will not be there in 12 months' time.

In the current coronavirus wasteland, the only oases to be found in recent weeks and months in town centres have been supermarkets, chemists and other essential stores with pubs, restaurants and cafes doing takeaways under the temporary PD rights introduced by the Town and Country Planning (General Permitted Development) (England) (Amendment) Order 2020 (SI 2020/330). Note: as set out in the title, this applies in England only – in Wales, Class A3 in the Use Classes Order still allows for the sale of "hot food for consumption off the premises".

At the time of writing, non-essential shops are on the point of reopening and so there will be some hesitant return to vitality in our town centres – although major question marks will remain over viability.

But post-coronavirus – whenever that happy time may be! – if workers (and their employers) have become completely habituated to carrying on their jobs from home, then why should their businesses want to keep up their tenancies in commercial premises? And if those premises are vacated, what is going to become of all those empty properties?

One option is to look to extend the permitted development rights for conversion of offices to encourage people to move back to the town from the suburbs. Although, based on recent experience, any new permitted development rights will need to have stricter standards.

And compare with this idea the recent "Planning for the Future" consultation launched in March 2020 which includes the suggestion of introducing new PD rights to allow empty buildings "to be demolished and replaced with well-designed new residential units which meet natural light standards".

If there is no extension of PD rights there will need to be a revision to the NPPF that provides positive encouragement for conversion provided certain conditions are met.

Interesting questions will arise in buildings without or flexibility to provide open space and suchlike but solutions would have to be found if our town centres are not to be left vacant. If people move back this will no doubt encourage small businesses like shops and cafes to start up.

But what of comparison shopping? Will people now be entirely converted to picking clothes or other goods on the basis of a computer image and description? Planning will have to deal with such a change in shopping patterns.

Will we see more sharing of space in edge of centre or out of town centres where bulky goods are on display or can be collected?

How do we plan for this?

What do we do about the need for more warehouse/distribution space?

We then start to come full circle when we consider how we are to plan transport infrastructure to cope with these new patterns of behaviour and trading.

Were those local authorities who bought shopping centres etc ahead of the game? Will they now be looking at other ways of using that property?

Telecommunications

Apart from the obvious joke about broadband becoming a human right there is a serious point behind it. There was recent guidance from DCMS which sought to require fibre broadband to be provided to every new property. Whether or not development can afford to do this is a moot point in the current environment. However, the market may decide that they have no choice as potential purchasers will want to know what is available.

Working from home has already had an impact on the use of the Internet. If the current level of usage is to remain then what needs to be done to provide what is required not just for homeowners but also for the good of the economy. We can only work from home if the technology permits us to do so.

The Telecoms Code is pretty one sided in favour of operators. We wonder whether the Government will feel the need to make it even more one sided to speed up the delivery of necessary infrastructure. That would have to be accompanied by a revision of the PD rights that operators currently enjoy. Interesting times ahead as those most affected by masts etc may not be that amused by the new rights whereas those who need connectivity will be pressing for quicker delivery.

Public inquiries

As noted above, the Planning Bar has been pushing various different models and trialling them. There are ongoing discussions with the Planning Inspectorate. Some think that this may be seen as an opportunity by the Inspectorate to further limit the attendance of lawyers in the system. Others see it as a means of speeding up decision making.

Whilst the technology works there are some practical issues. For example, at the moment, notes cannot immediately be passed between Counsel and solicitor/professional accessor or expert witness because they are not able to sit next to each other, i.e. that is not so easy if you are engaged in a virtual Inquiry. There is already plenty out there on Linkedin and other sites where those who have tried this have set out the issues and how they can be overcome.

One solution is for each side to have a Whatsapp group where notes can be passed in real time.

Conducting cross-examination over a video link will be a new skill for advocates to master, although it is already an arrangement made use of in other courts.

For the Inspector there will be the added issue of keeping an eye on who wishes to speak or interrupt. The Inspector would no doubt have to be in charge of muting/unmuting audio. This would add pressure to ensure that interruptions could be accommodated where appropriate e.g. a necessary interruption by Counsel on a point of law etc.

The Courts seem to have dealt with this and there are a number of examples of virtual JRs and even a trial in the Court of Protection. Indeed, the Planning Court seems by now to be functioning more or less normally with virtual hearings (which do not of course generally involve the hearing of live evidence or the cross-examination of witnesses).

One thing topical issue that has been brought to a head by the current situation is the need for site visits for appeals. Clearly, there does not need to be a site visit in every case. For example, do we need a site visit for Certificate of Lawfulness appeals because probably in most cases one is concerned with the historical facts or the applicable law and very rarely does the appeal turn on a site visit.

For a regular planning appeal, the Inspector could use Google Earth or some similar app. This change may be forced on us as the Inspectorate will need to find a way to deal with the backlog of appeals. Indeed, a Planning Inspectorate news item of 28 April 2020 records that "a trial of 'virtual site visits' is underway involving thirteen Inspectors", see at https://www.gov.uk/government/news/planning-inspectorate-casework-continues-as-first-pilot-digital-hearing-to-take-place-in-may

Or if a site visit was essential for a proper determination of the appeal then that could be justified as a reasonable necessity under lockdown, with steps taken in advance for the parties to ensure that the

Inspector looks at everything they want him or her to look at and then carry it out unaccompanied.

All in all there are a number of challenges ahead and it is hard to know where we will end up.

The future?

Given the recent changes in attitudes to and regulations for lock-down, it is hard to know how things will pan out over the coming weeks and months. At the time of writing, consultation is being mooted for an introduction of "zonal planning" or the creation of special development zones where planning rules will be relaxed in hope of fast-tracking development – but obviously considerable care will be required to ensure that quality of development is not sacrificed on the altar of progressing development speedily. Will we back to normal any time soon? And what will "normal" look like?

MORE BOOKS BY LAW BRIEF PUBLISHING

A selection of our other titles available now:-

'How to Be a Freelance Solicitor: A Practical Guide to the SRA-Regulated Freelance Solicitor Model' by Paul Bennett
'A Practical Guide to Prison Injury Claims' by Malcolm Johnson
'A Practical Guide to the Small Claims Track' by Dominic Bright
'A Practical Guide to Advising Clients at the Police Station' by Colin Stephen McKeown-Beaumont
'A Practical Guide to Antisocial Behaviour Injunctions' by Iain Wightwick
'Practical Mediation: A Guide for Mediators, Advocates, Advisers, Lawyers, and Students in Civil, Commercial, Business, Property, Workplace, and Employment Cases' by Jonathan Dingle with John Sephton
'The Mini-Pupillage Workbook' by David Boyle
'A Practical Guide to Crofting Law' by Brian Inkster
'A Practical Guide to Spousal Maintenance' by Liz Cowell
'A Practical Guide to the Law of Domain Names and Cybersquatting' by Andrew Clemson
'A Practical Guide to the Law of Gender Pay Gap Reporting' by Harini Iyengar
'A Practical Guide to the Rights of Grandparents in Children Proceedings' by Stuart Barlow
'NHS Whistleblowing and the Law' by Joseph England
'Employment Law and the Gig Economy' by Nigel Mackay & Annie Powell
'A Practical Guide to Noise Induced Hearing Loss (NIHL) Claims' by Andrew Mckie, Ian Skeate, Gareth McAloon
'An Introduction to Beauty Negligence Claims – A Practical Guide for the Personal Injury Practitioner' by Greg Almond
'Intercompany Agreements for Transfer Pricing Compliance' by Paul Sutton
'Zen and the Art of Mediation' by Martin Plowman
'A Practical Guide to the SRA Principles, Individual and Law Firm Codes of Conduct 2019 – What Every Law Firm Needs to Know' by Paul Bennett
'A Practical Guide to Adoption for Family Lawyers' by Graham Pegg
'A Practical Guide to Industrial Disease Claims' by Andrew Mckie & Ian Skeate
'A Practical Guide to Redundancy' by Philip Hyland
'A Practical Guide to Vicarious Liability' by Mariel Irvine

‘A Practical Guide to Applications for Landlord’s Consent and Variation of Leases’ by Mark Shelton

‘A Practical Guide to Relief from Sanctions Post-Mitchell and Denton’ by Peter Causton

‘A Practical Guide to Equity Release for Advisors’ by Paul Sams

‘A Practical Guide to Unlawful Eviction and Harassment’ by Stephanie Lovegrove

‘A Practical Guide to the Law Relating to Food’ by Ian Thomas

‘A Practical Guide to Financial Services Claims’ by Chris Hegarty

‘The Law of Houses in Multiple Occupation: A Practical Guide to HMO Proceedings’ by Julian Hunt

‘A Practical Guide to Unlawful Eviction and Harassment’ by Stephanie Lovegrove

‘A Practical Guide to Solicitor and Client Costs’ by Robin Dunne

‘Occupiers, Highways and Defective Premises Claims: A Practical Guide Post-Jackson – 2nd Edition’ by Andrew Mckie

‘A Practical Guide to Financial Ombudsman Service Claims’ by Adam Temple & Robert Scrivenor

‘A Practical Guide to the Law of Enfranchisement and Lease Extension’ by Paul Sams

‘A Practical Guide to Marketing for Lawyers – 2nd Edition’ by Catherine Bailey & Jennet Ingram

'A Practical Guide to Advising Schools on Employment Law' by Jonathan Holden

‘A Practical Guide to Running Housing Disrepair and Cavity Wall Claims: 2nd Edition’ by Andrew Mckie & Ian Skeate

‘A Practical Guide to Holiday Sickness Claims – 2nd Edition’ by Andrew Mckie & Ian Skeate

‘Arguments and Tactics for Personal Injury and Clinical Negligence Claims’ by Dorian Williams

‘A Practical Guide to QOCS and Fundamental Dishonesty’ by James Bentley

‘A Practical Guide to Drone Law’ by Rufus Ballaster, Andrew Firman, Eleanor Clot

‘A Practical Guide to Compliance for Personal Injury Firms Working With Claims Management Companies’ by Paul Bennett

‘A Practical Guide to the Landlord and Tenant Act 1954: Commercial Tenancies’ by Richard Hayes & David Sawtell

www.ingramcontent.com/pod-product-compliance
Lightning Source LLC
LaVergne TN
LVHW022318200926
848481LV00004B/1373
* 9 7 8 1 9 1 3 7 1 5 1 4 4 *